Christmas is coming!

Cross off the days till Santa arrives

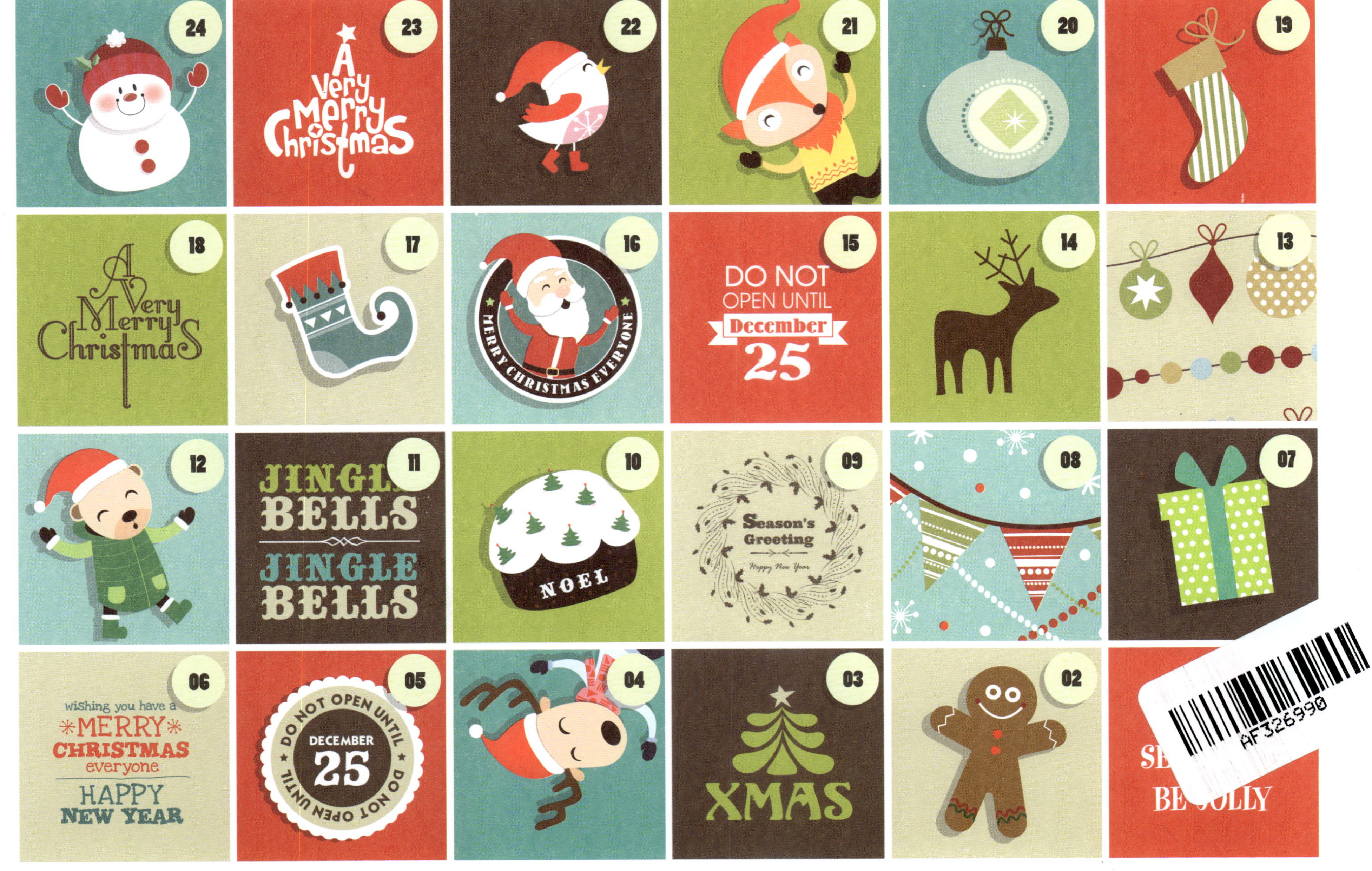

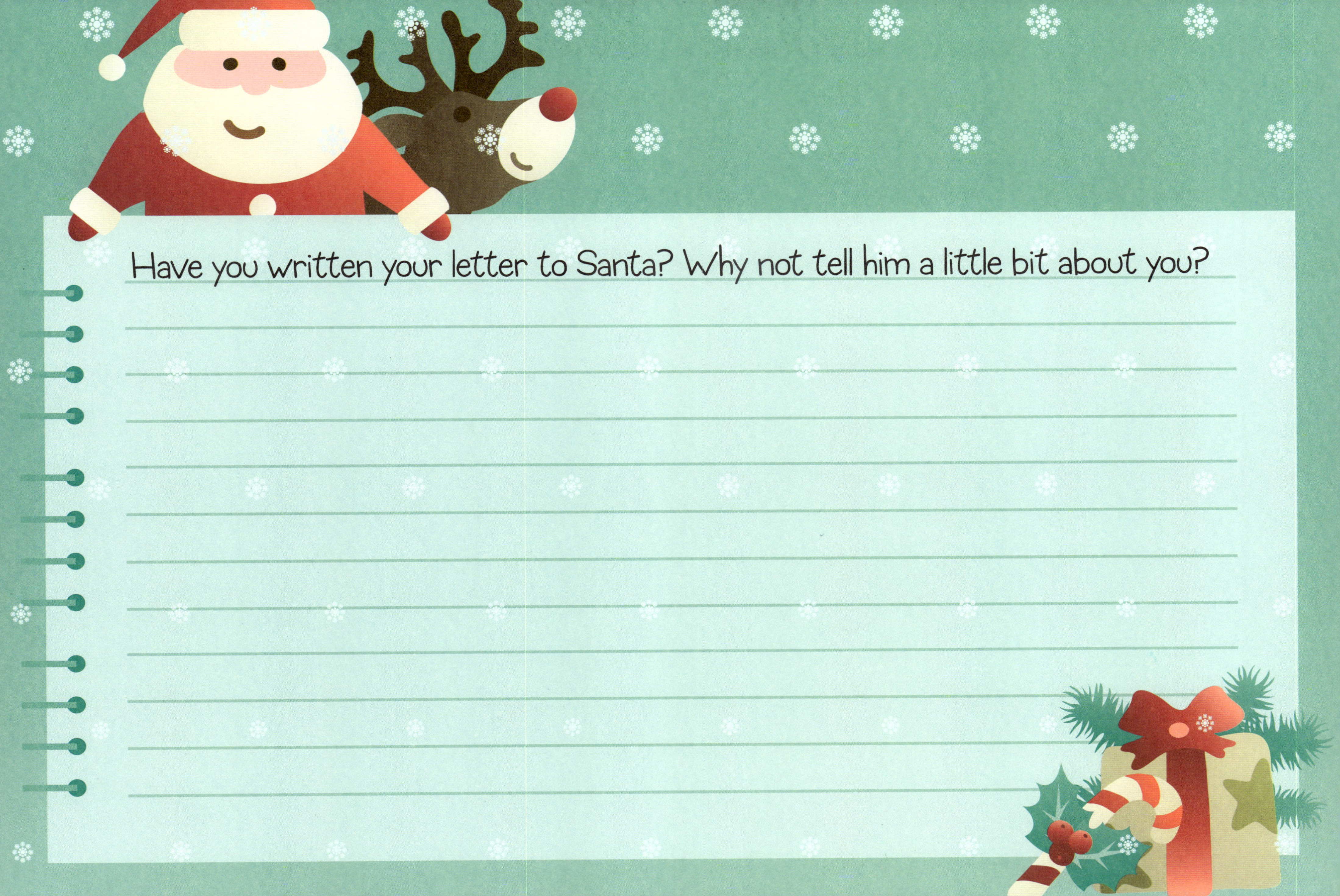
Have you written your letter to Santa? Why not tell him a little bit about you?

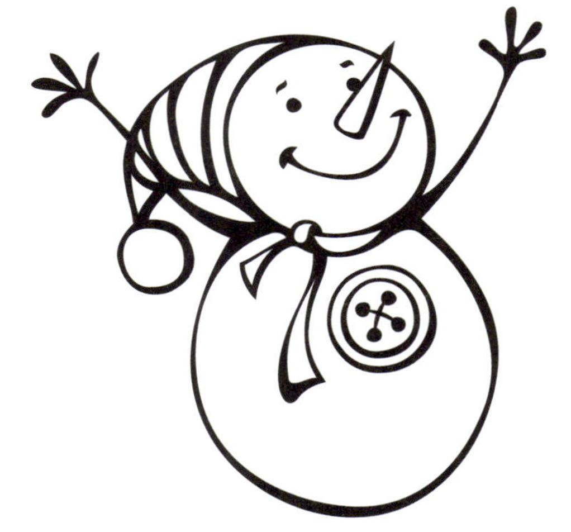
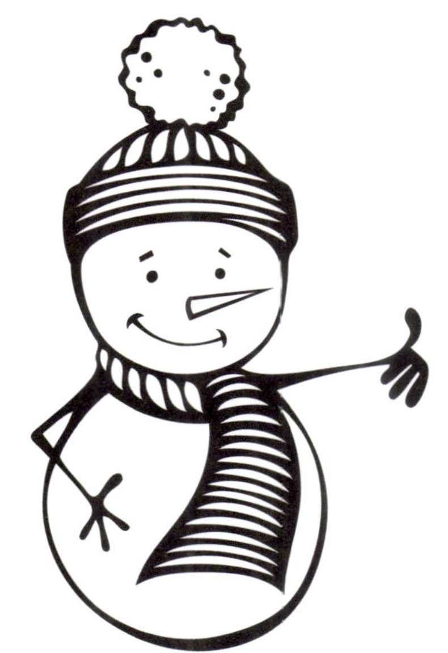
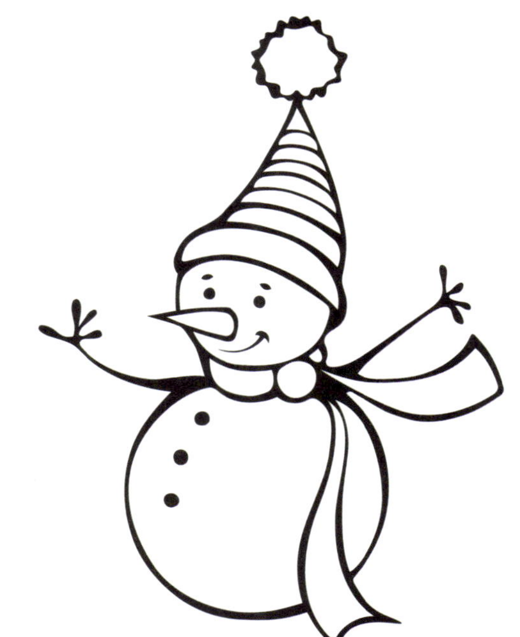

Colour in the snowmen

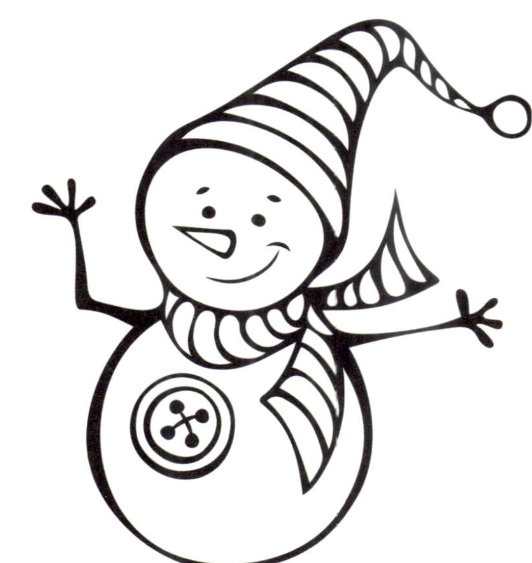
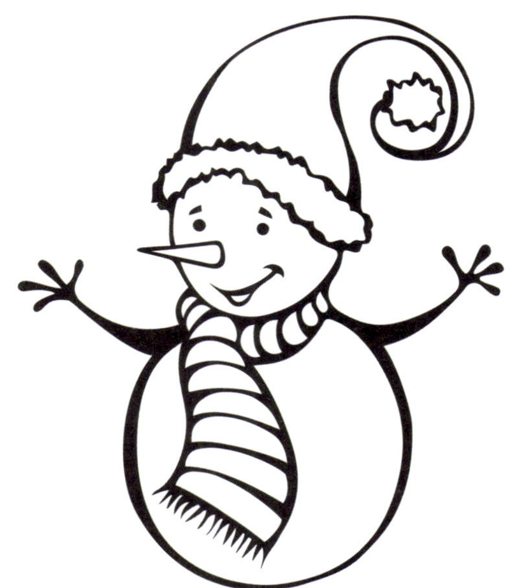

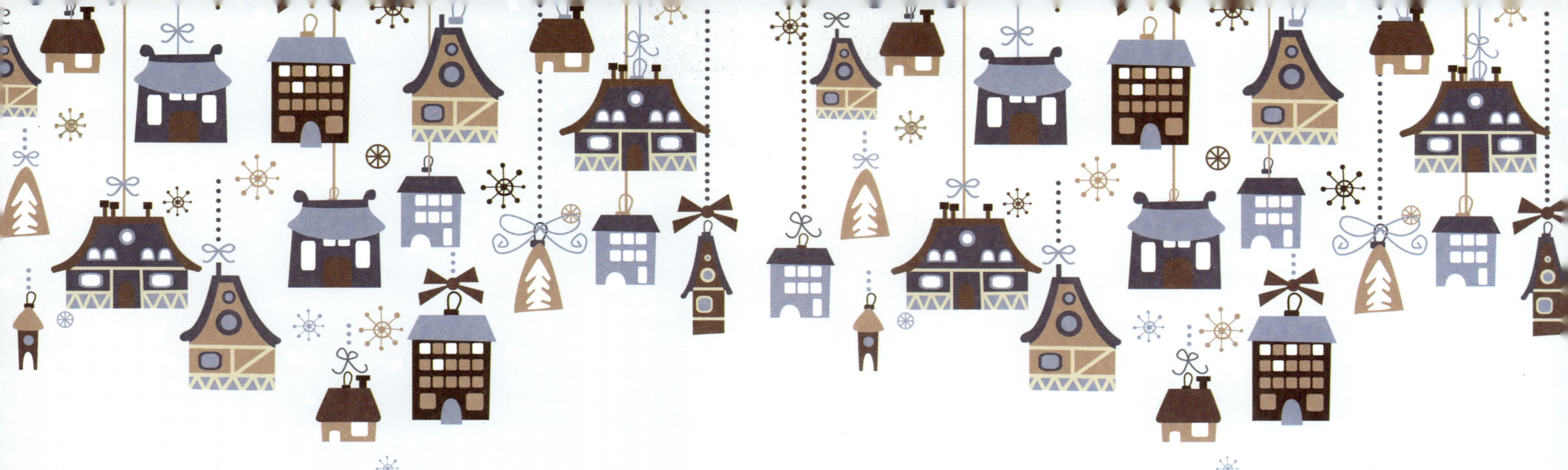

Draw your favourite thing about Christmas

Don't forget to mail your letter to Santa! Decorate the envelope with some Christmas stamps.

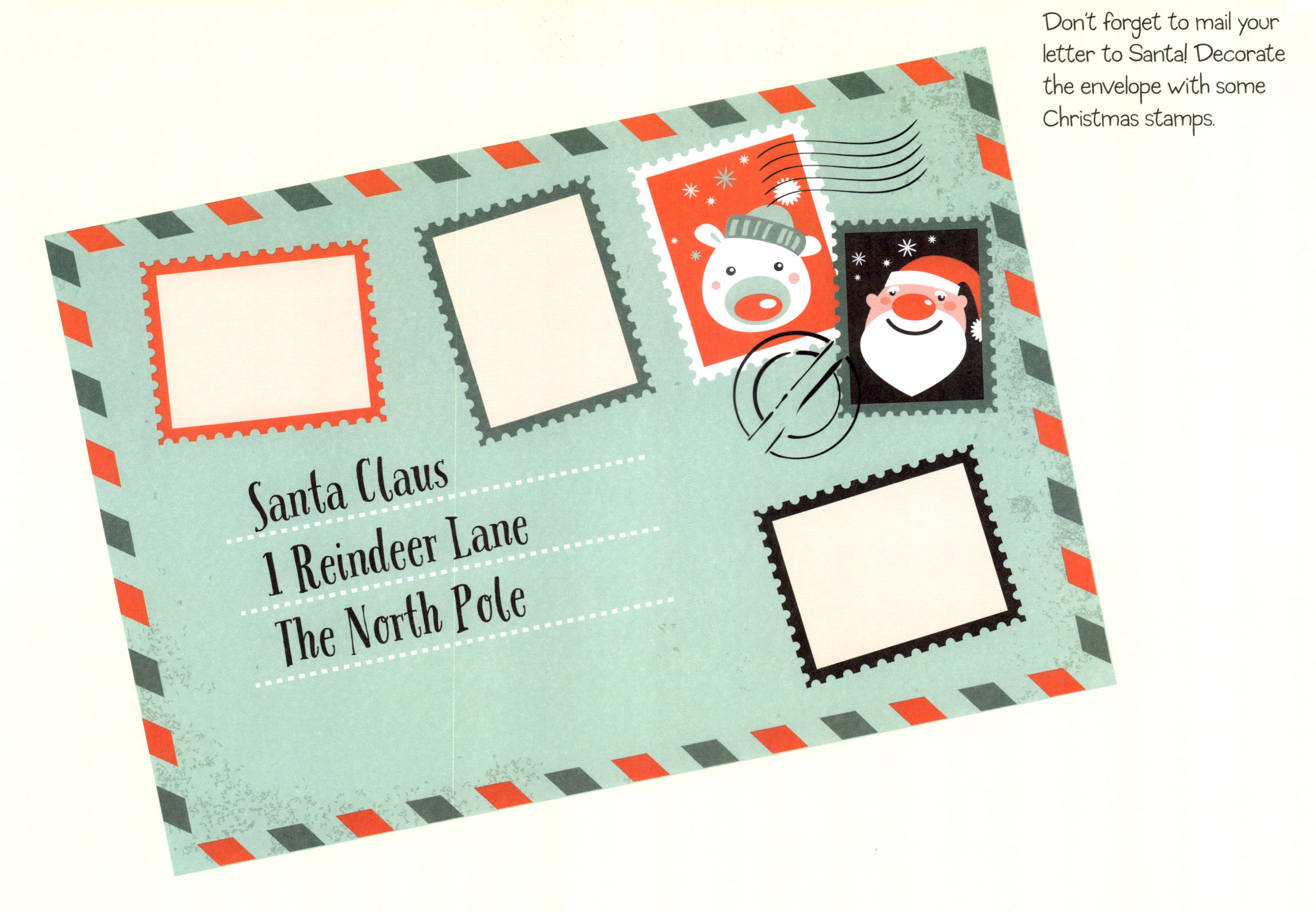
Santa Claus
1 Reindeer Lane
The North Pole

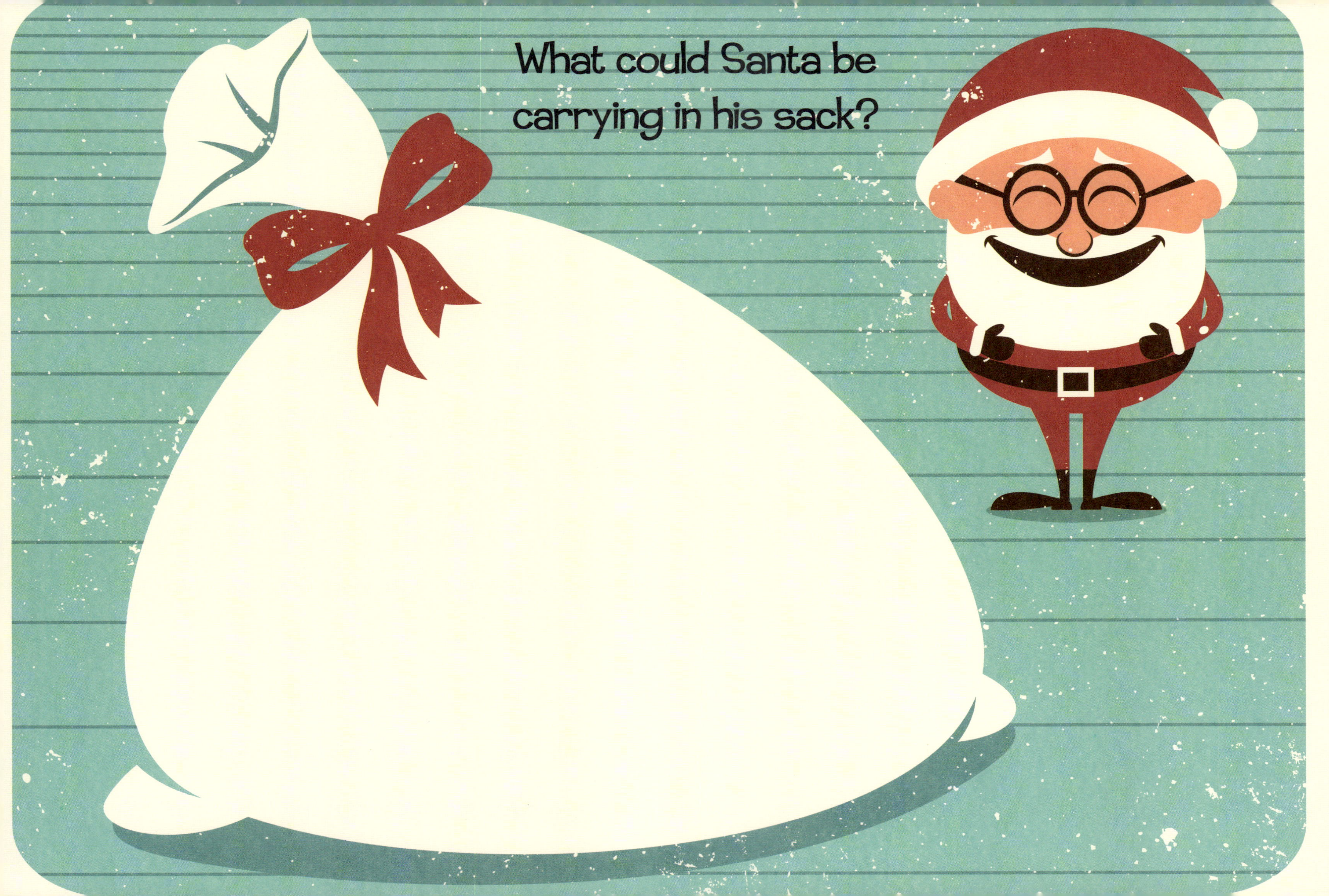
What could Santa be carrying in his sack?

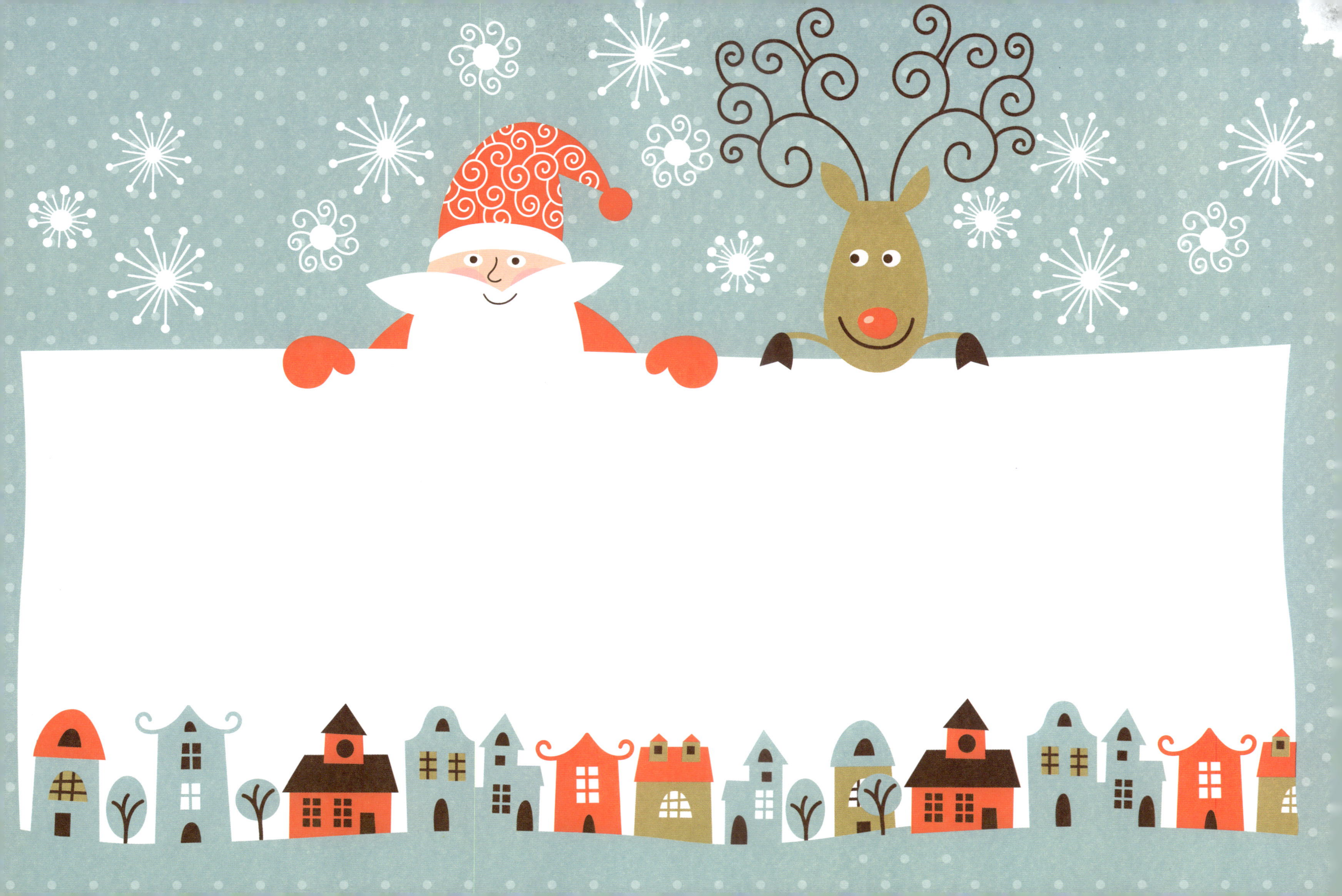

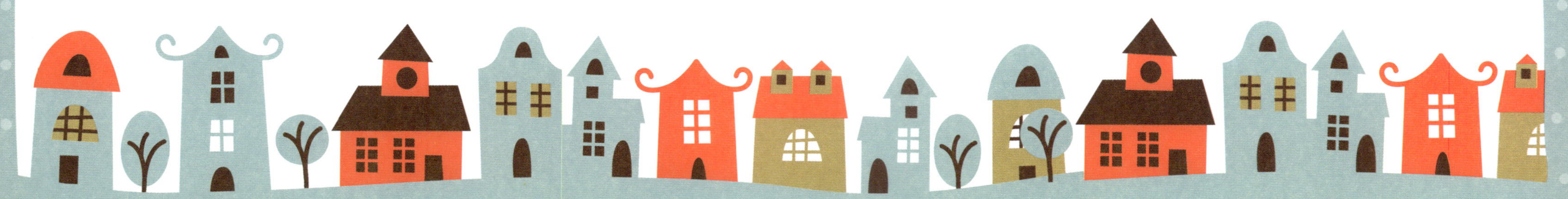

Create your own fun paper! Colour in the page in your best Christmas colours.

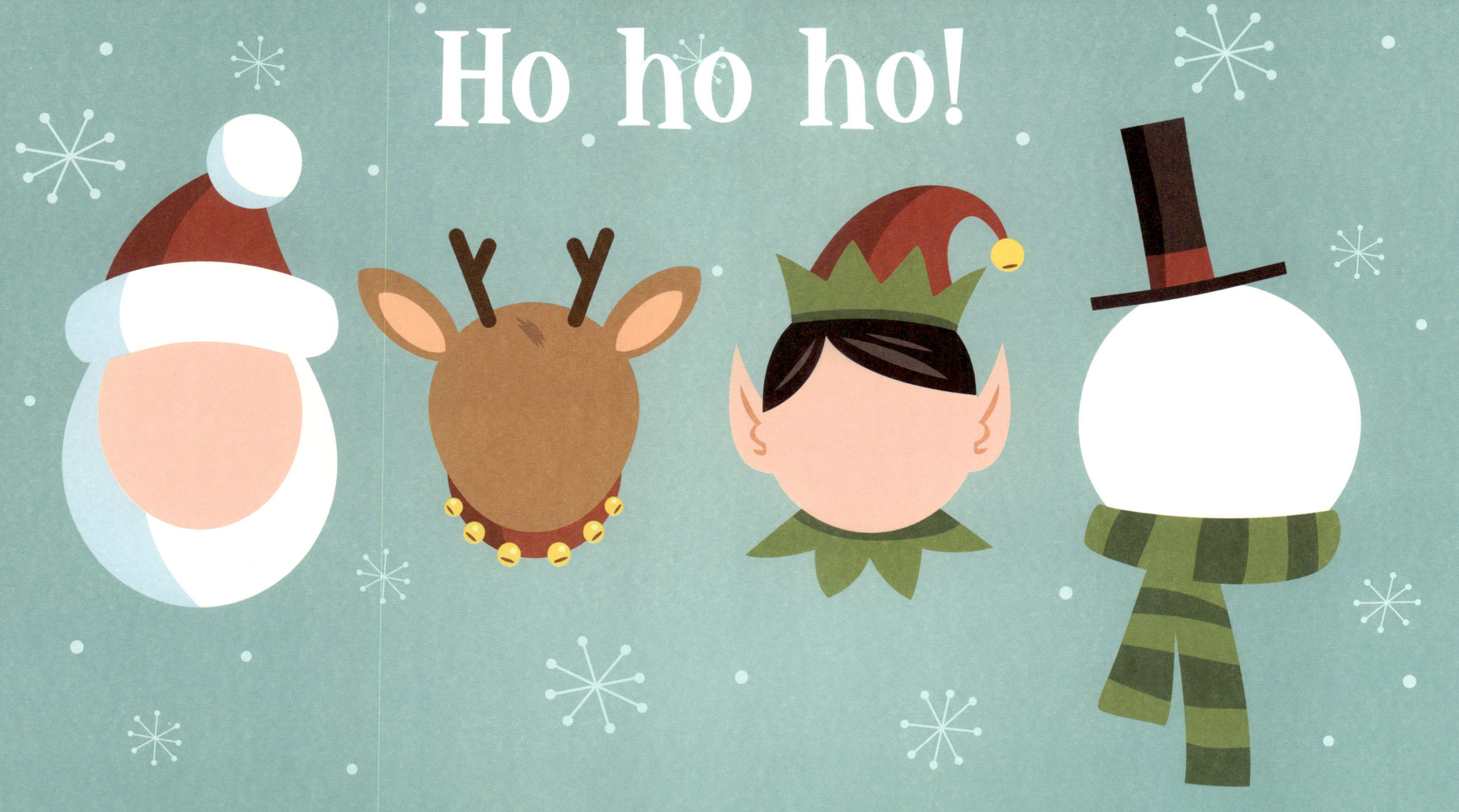

Ho ho ho!
Everyone is getting into the Christmas spirit!
Draw your family in the funny Christmas faces.

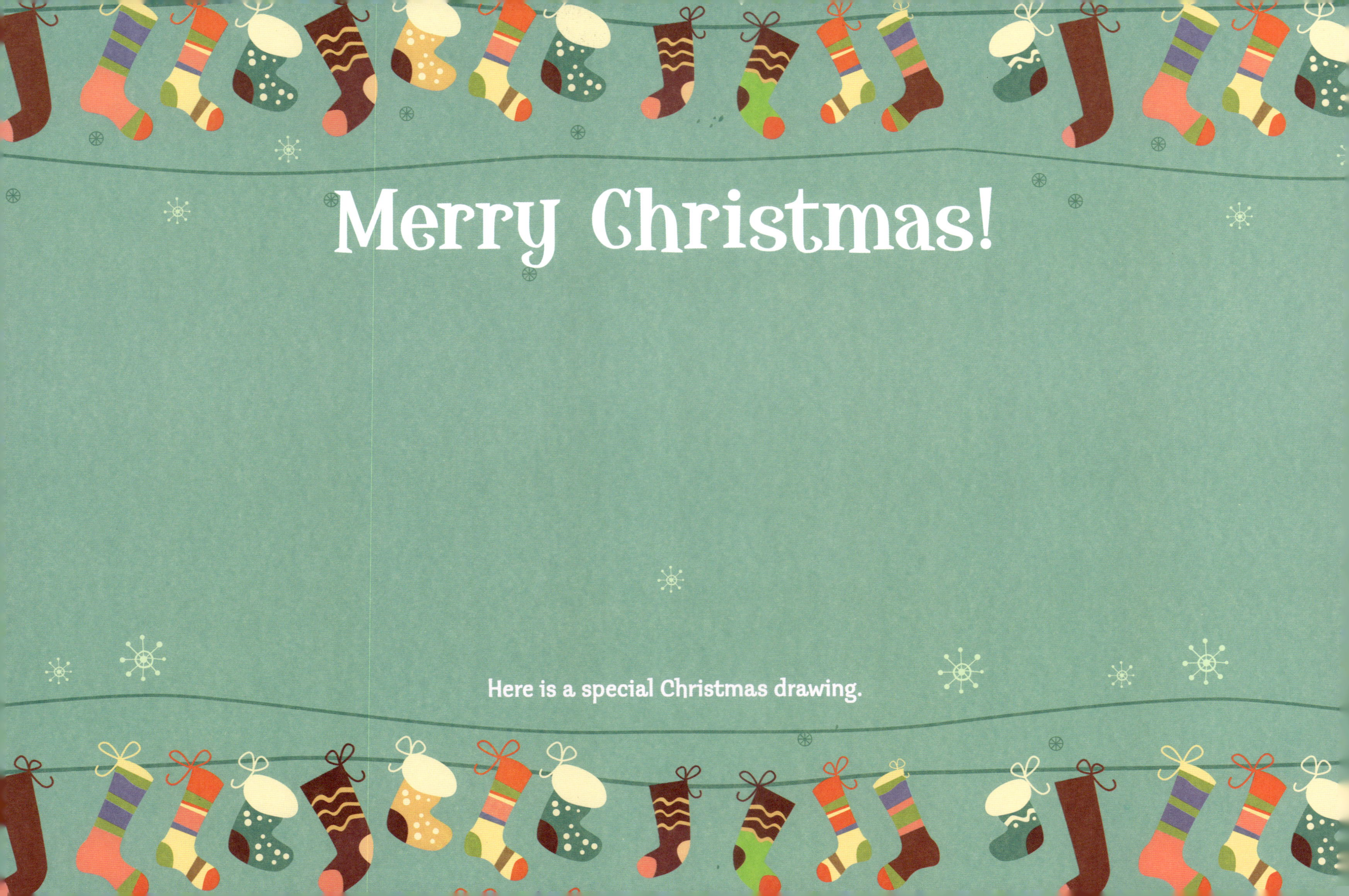
Merry Christmas!
Here is a special Christmas drawing.

Happy holidays!

Write or draw some Christmas messages for your family.

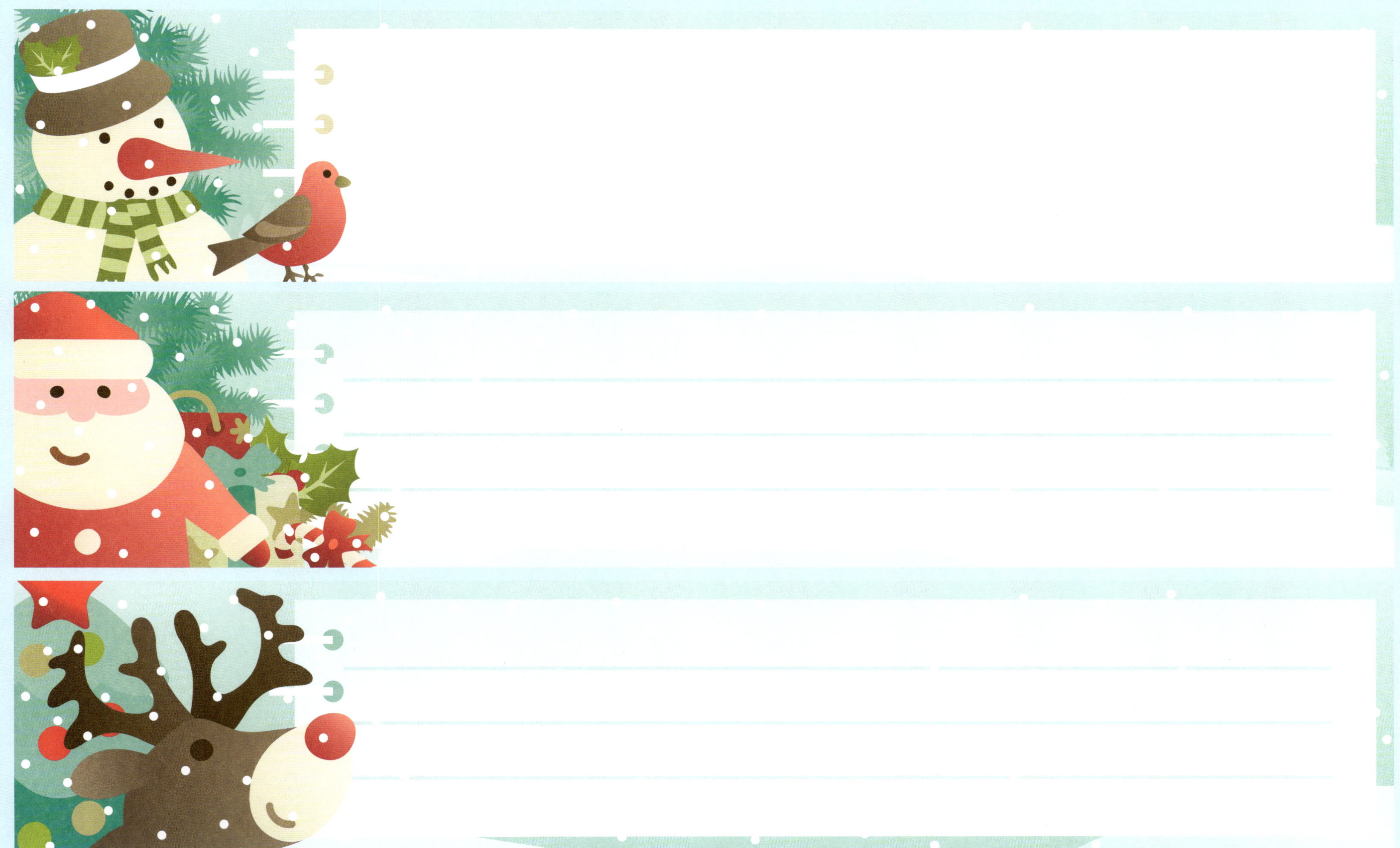

MERRY CHRISTMAS

Colour in the Santa and tree!

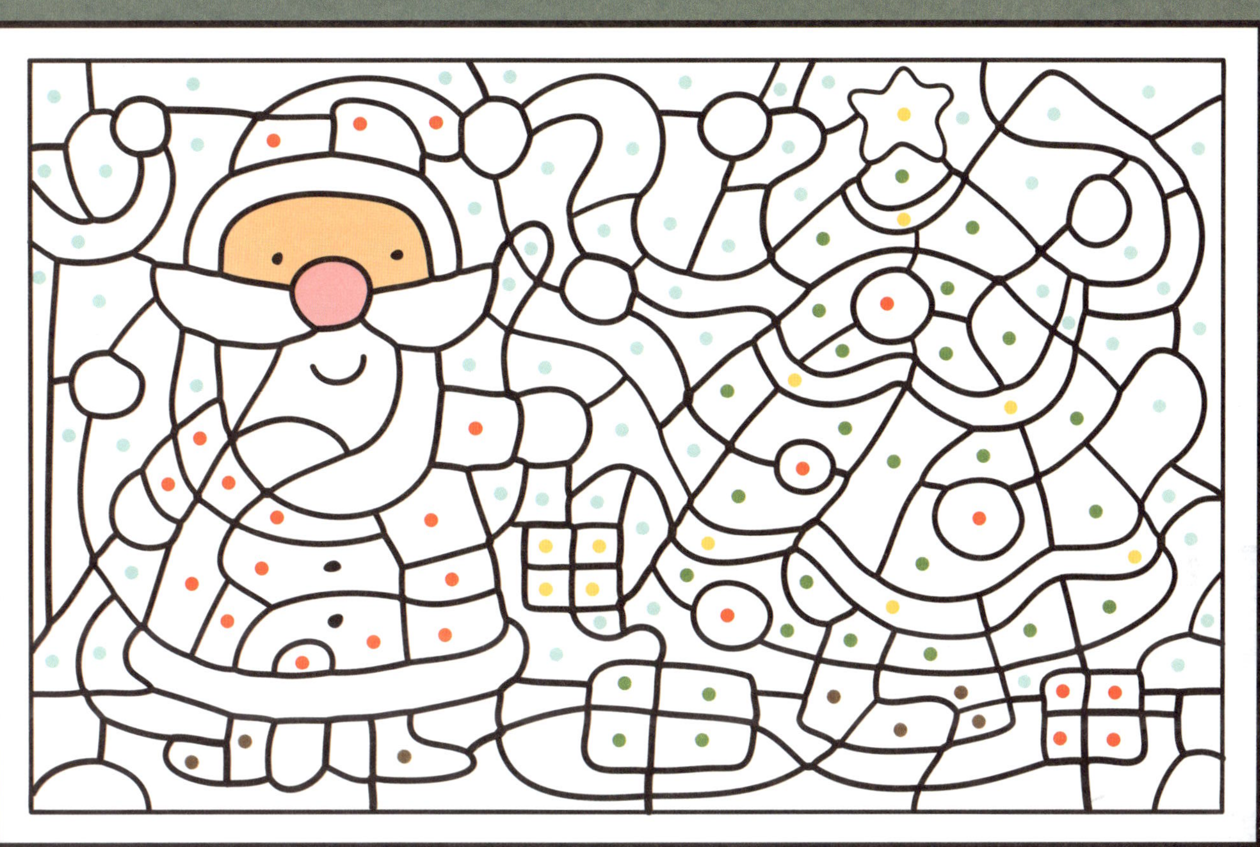

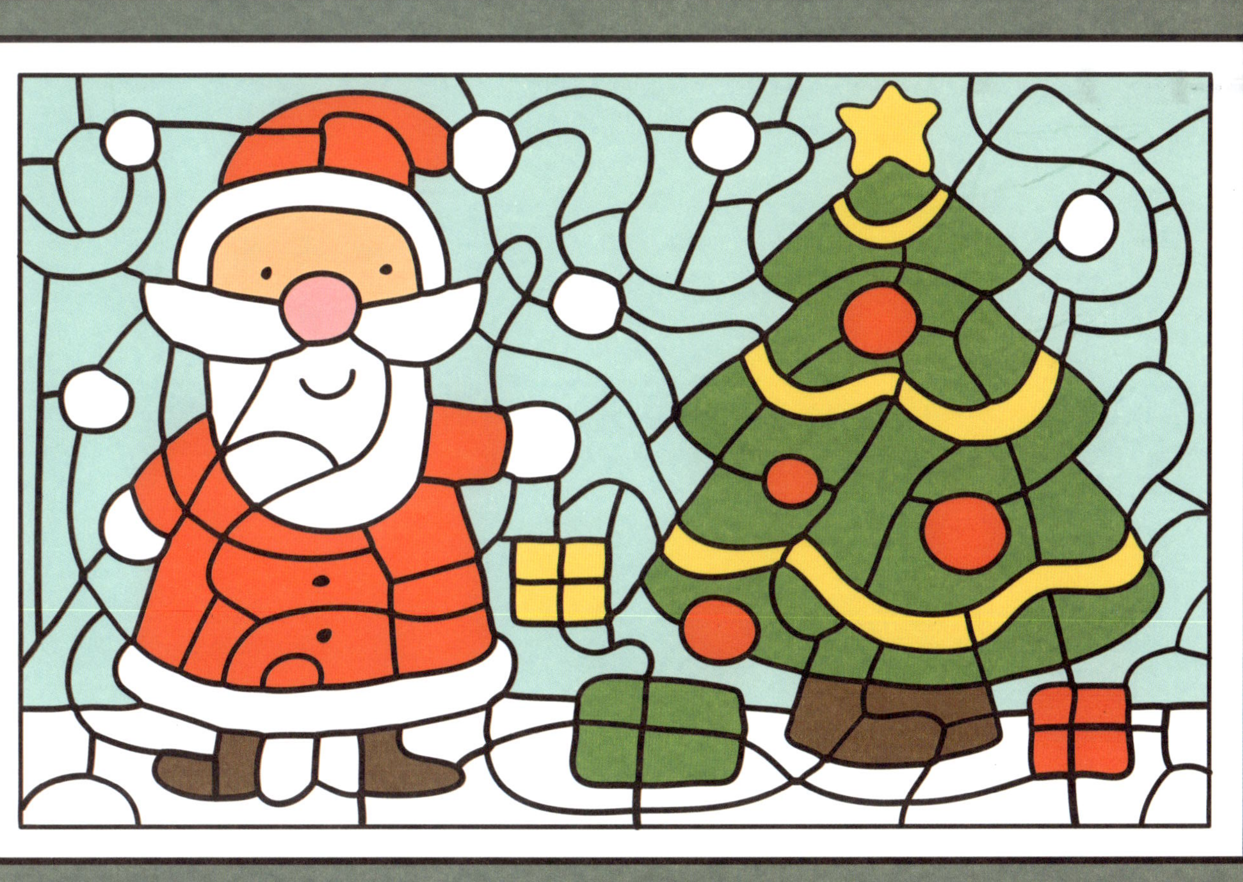

Jingle bells!

Christmas is on its way!

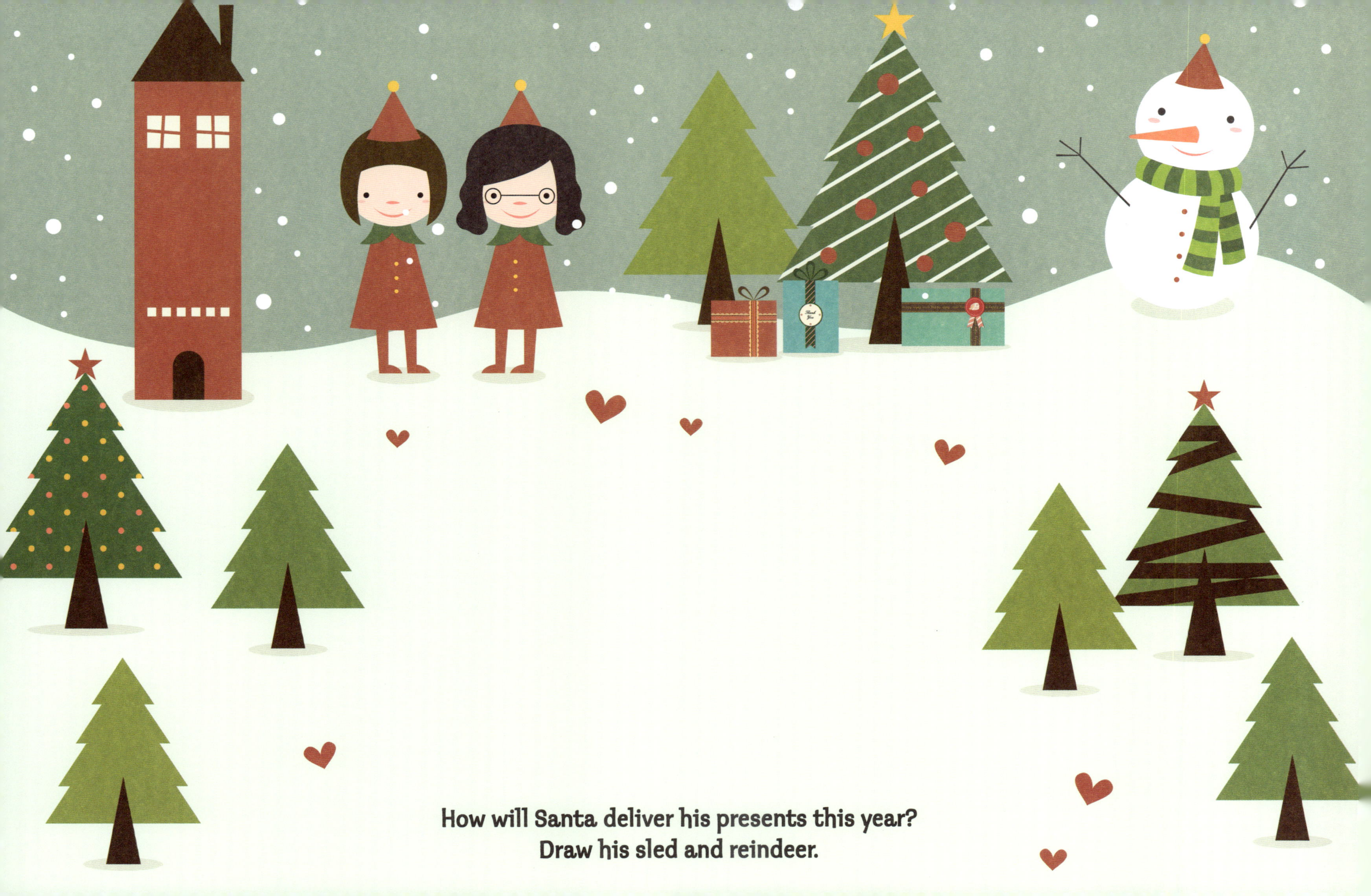
How will Santa deliver his presents this year?
Draw his sled and reindeer.

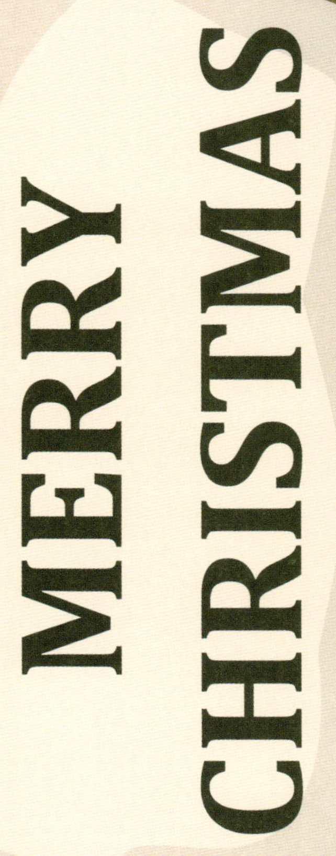

MERRY CHRISTMAS

Is Santa bringing presents to your friends this year? Fill in Santa's Christmas list.

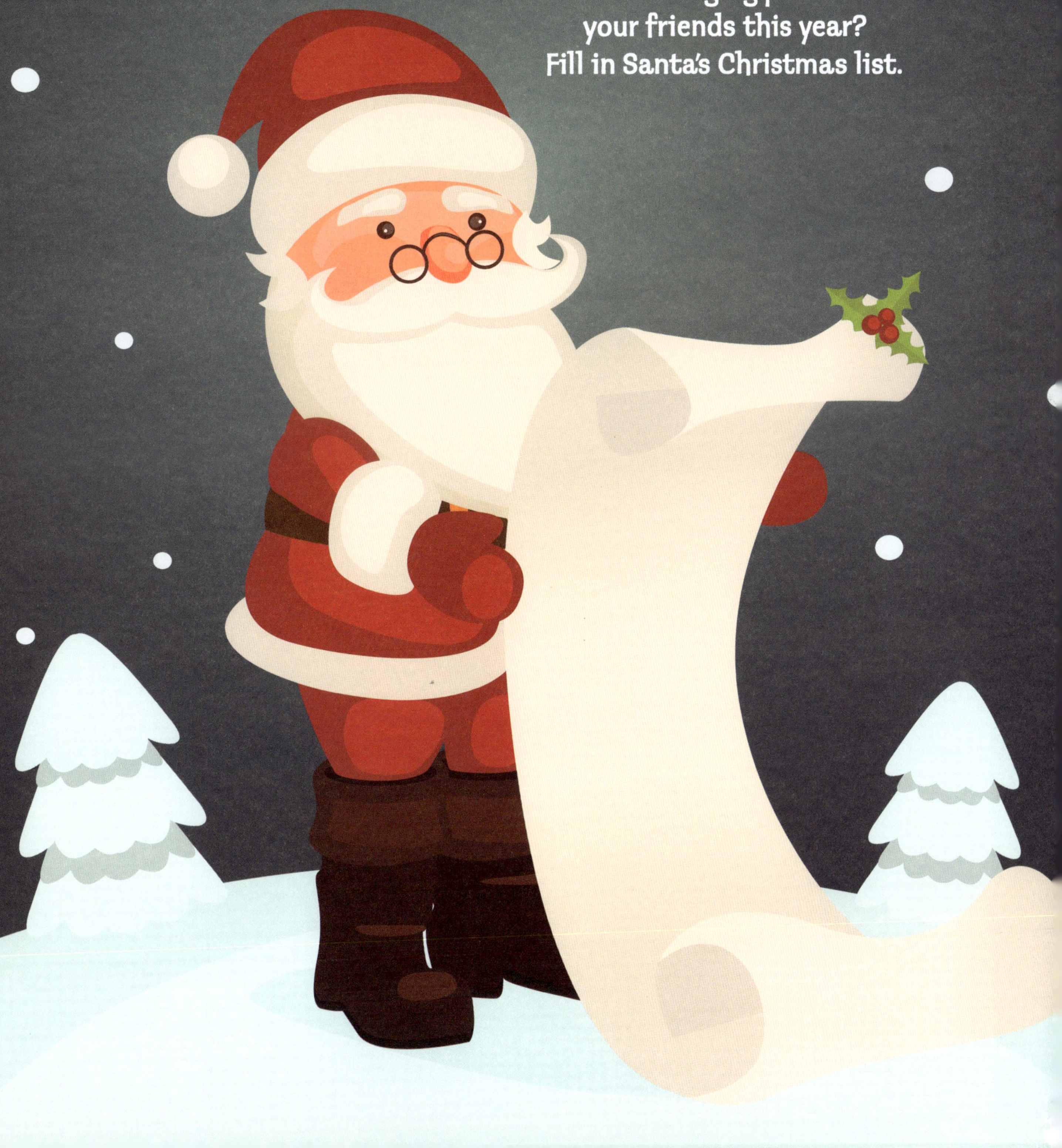

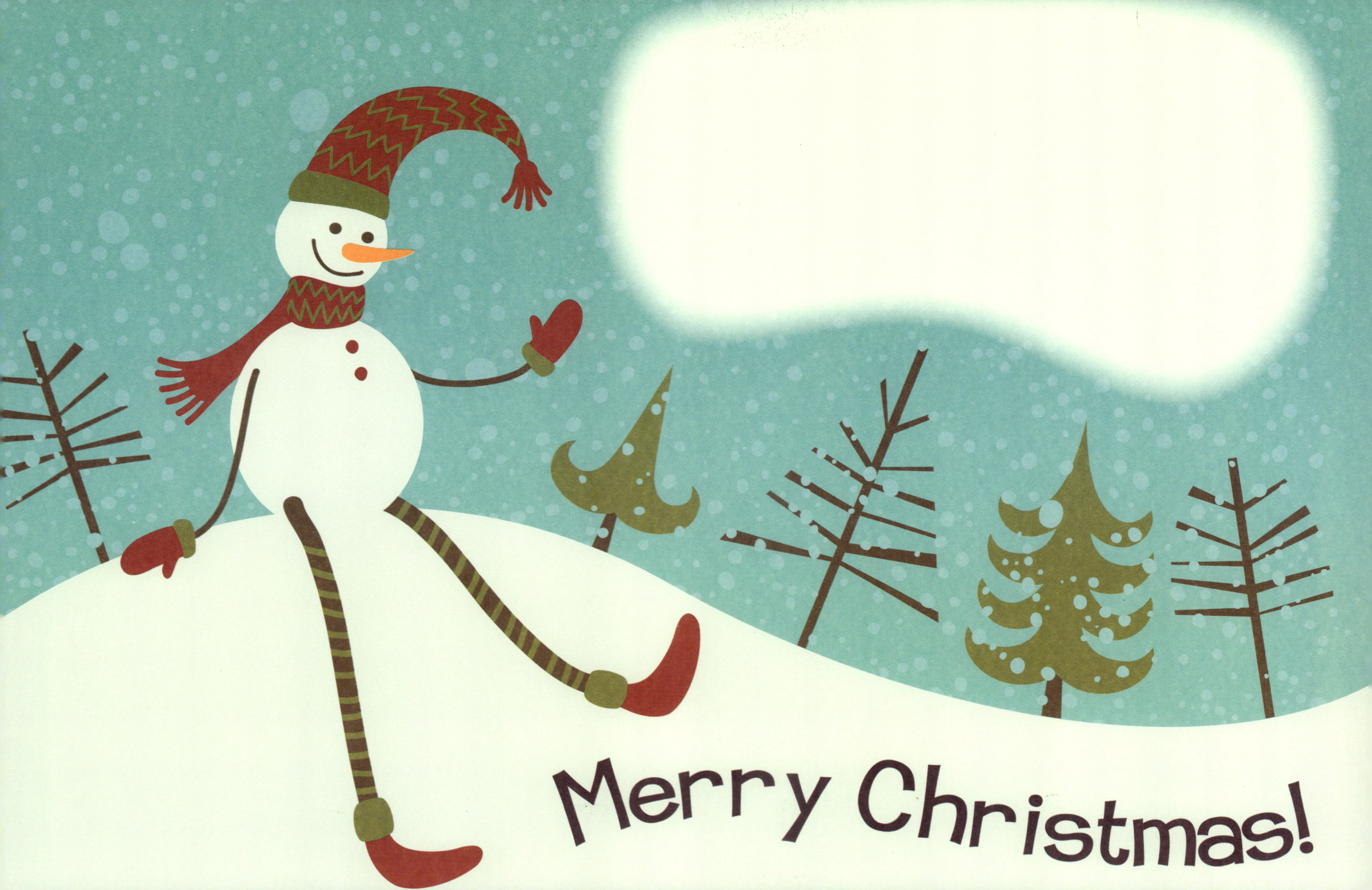
Merry Christmas!

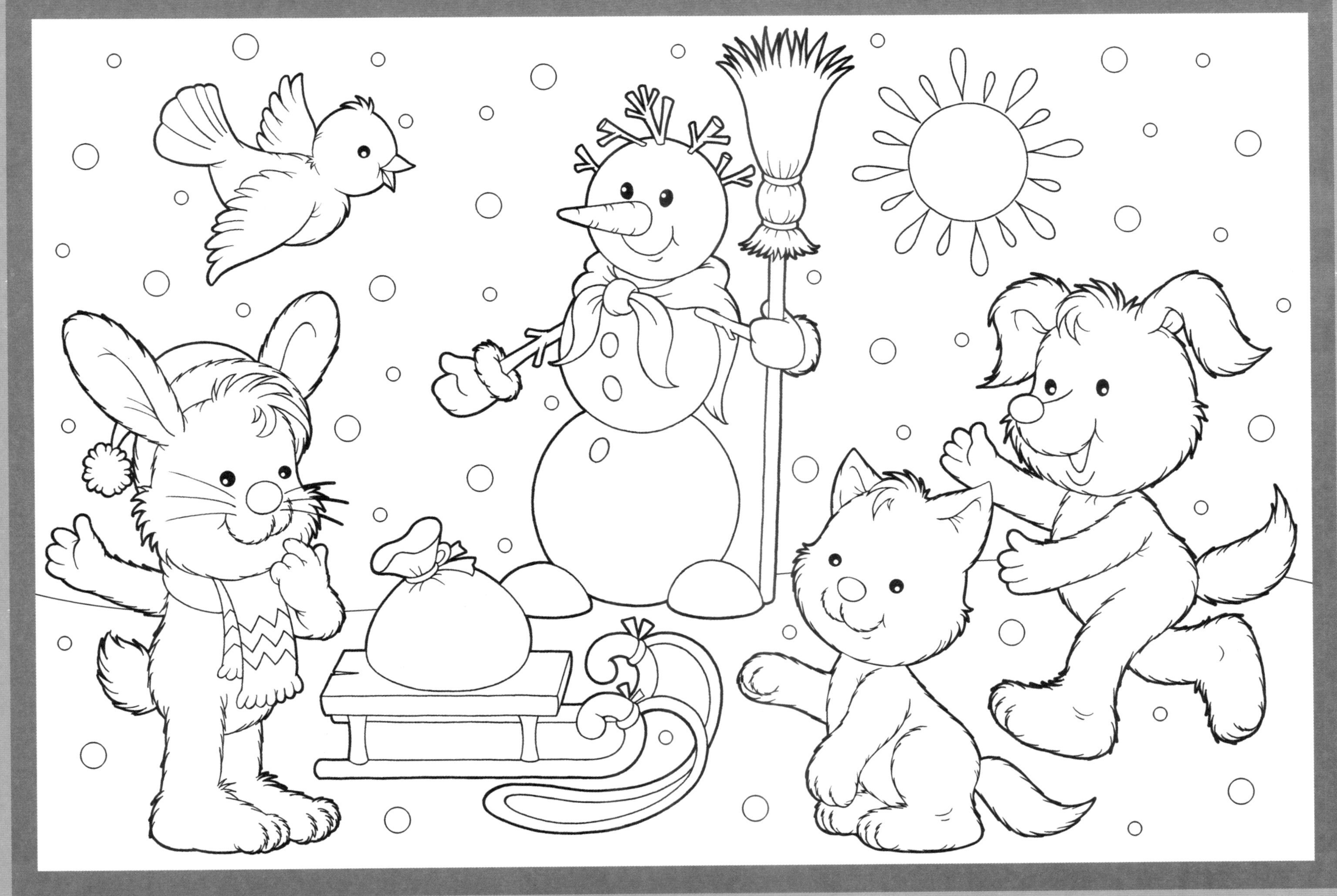

Some Christmas drawings and messages for my family!

Have you decorated your house?

Draw a picture of it here.

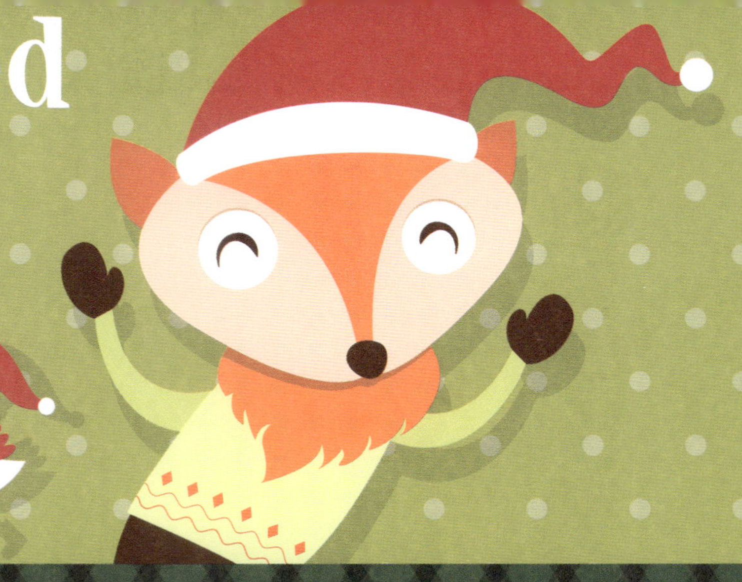

Decorate the Christmas puddings!

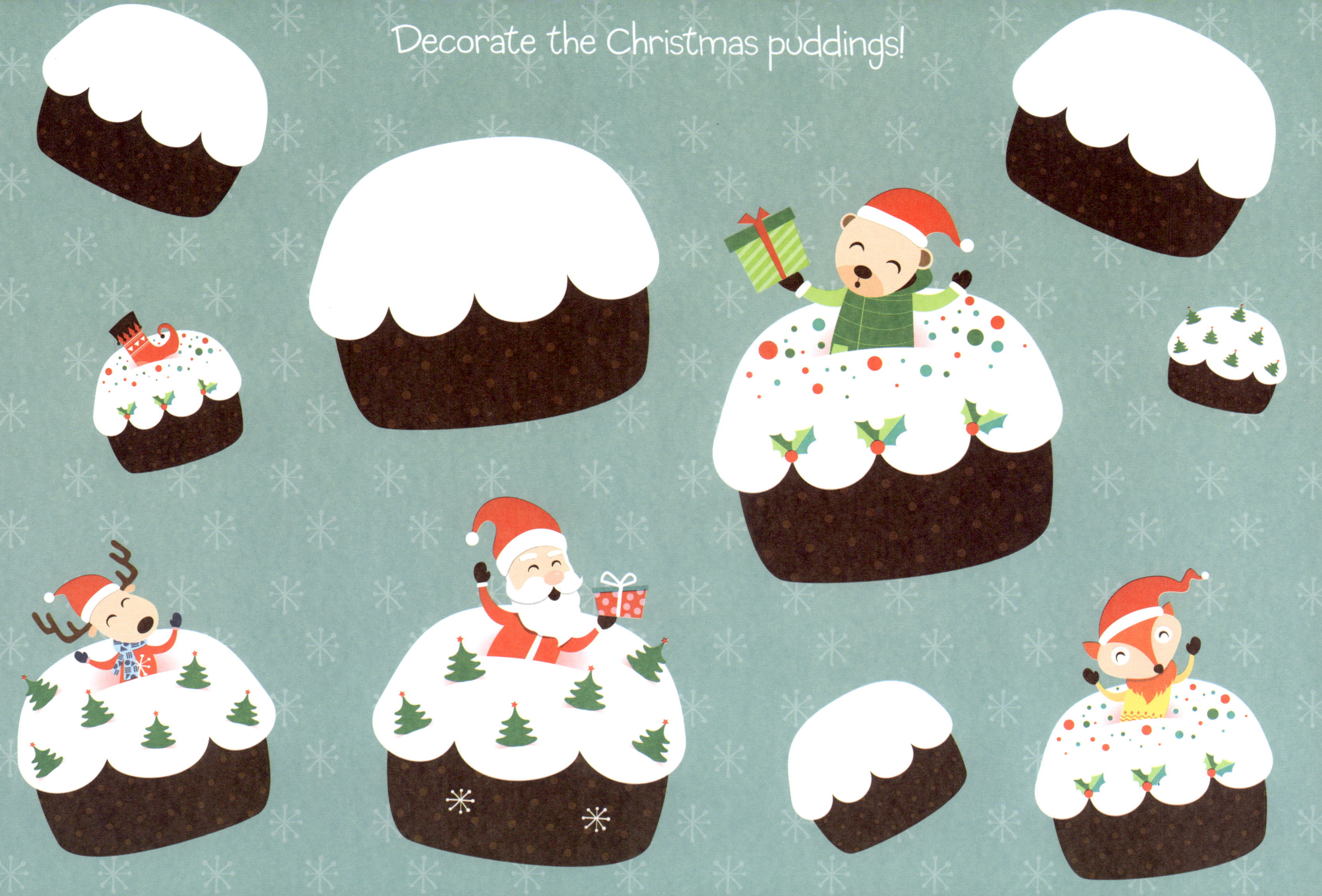

The Twelve Days of Christmas!

a partridge in a pear tree

two turtle doves

three French hens

four calling birds

five gold rings

six geese a-laying

seven swans a-swimming

eight maids a-milking

nine ladies dancing

ten lords a-leaping

eleven pipers piping

twelve drummers drumming

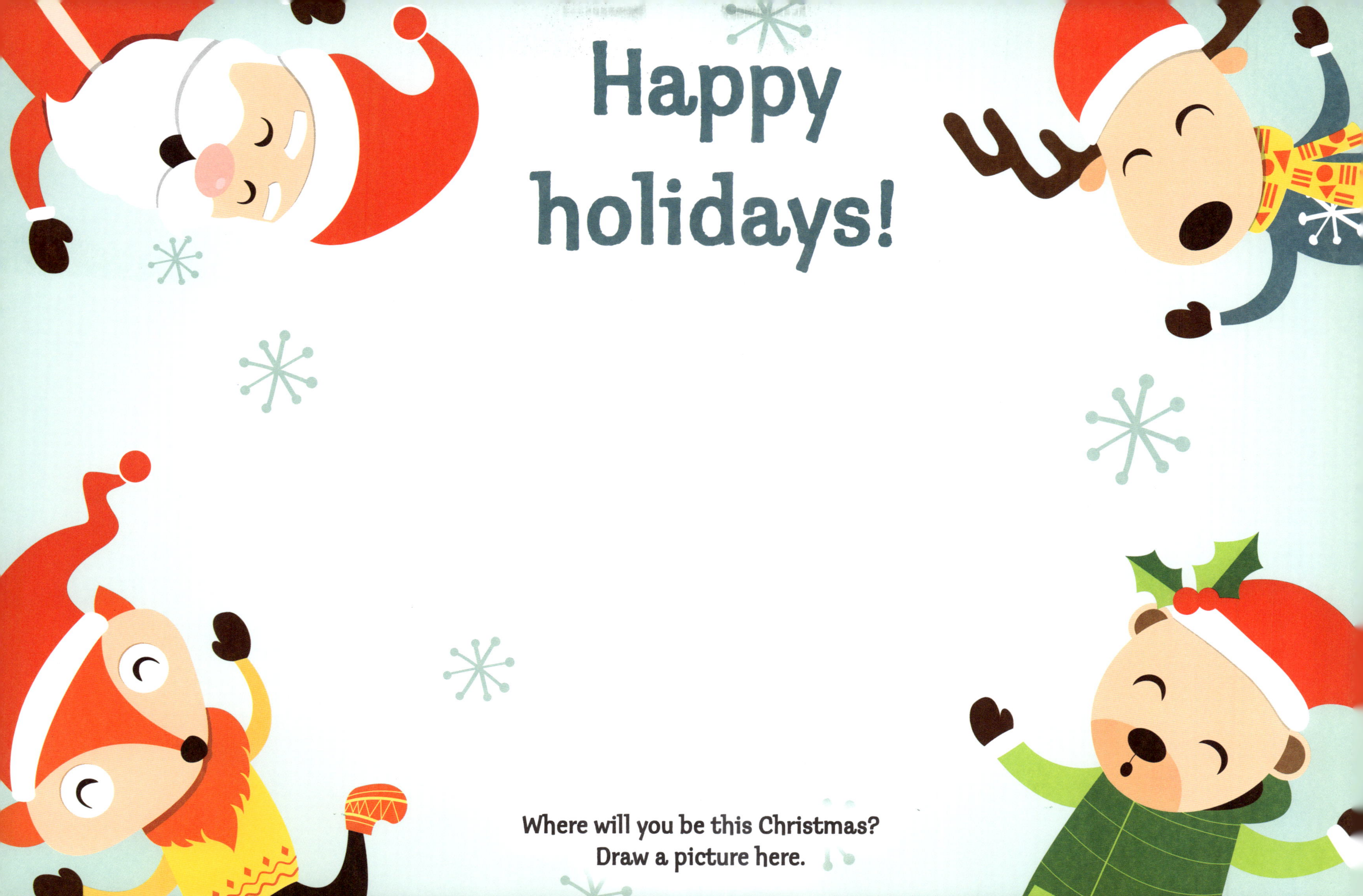

Happy holidays!
Where will you be this Christmas?
Draw a picture here.

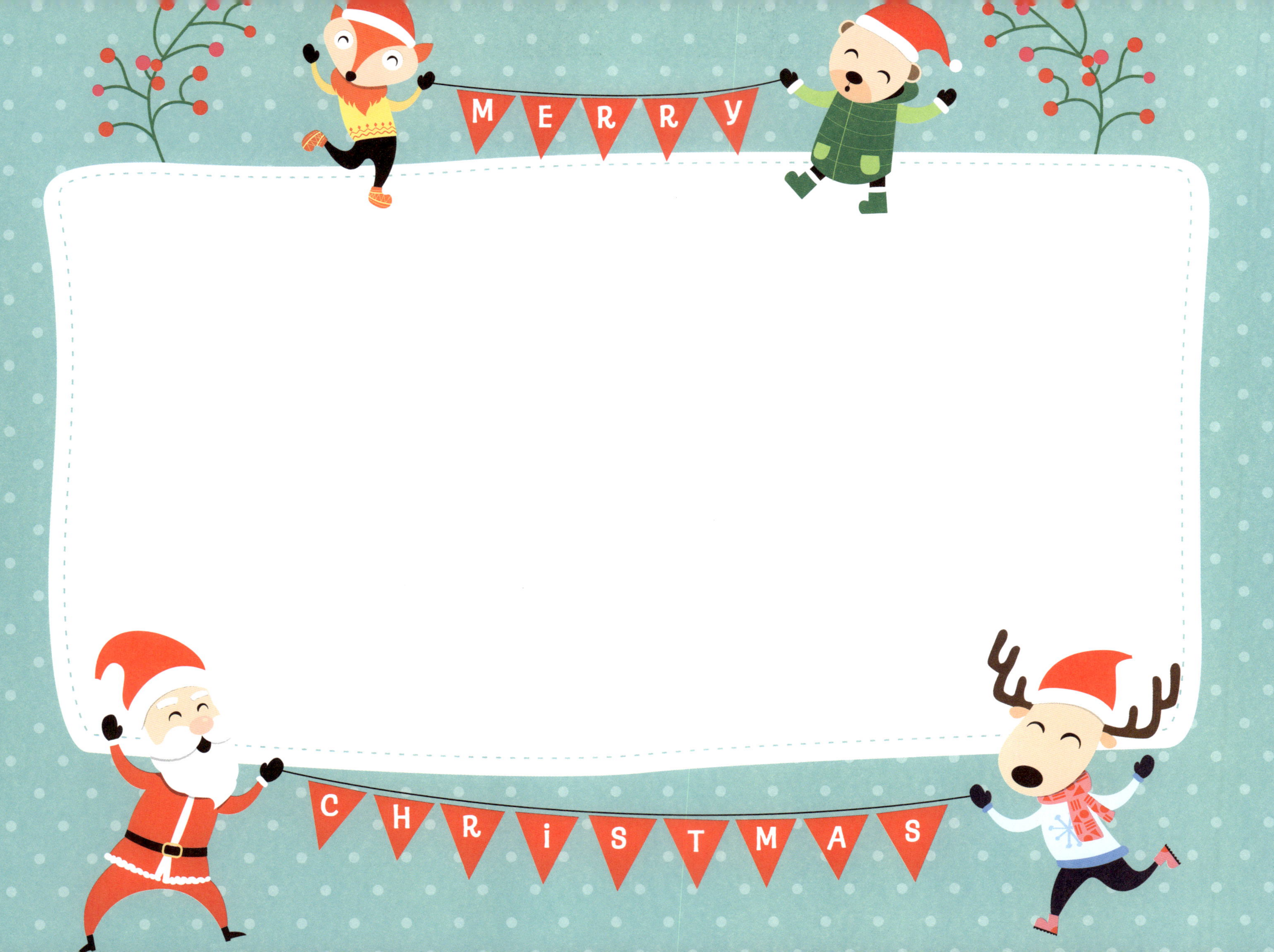

MERRY
CHRISTMAS

Finish colouring in the pictures to make special Christmas paper!

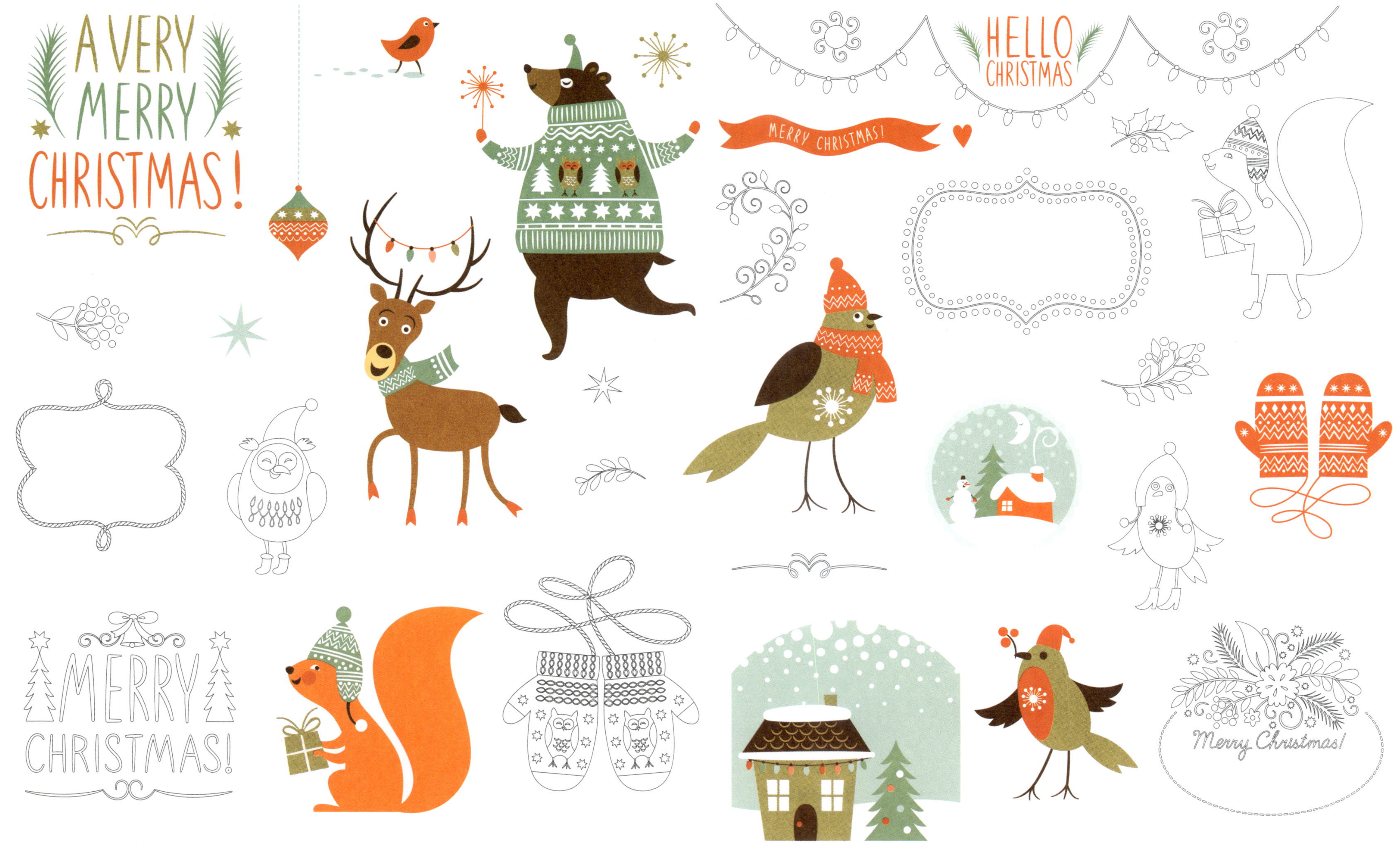

A VERY MERRY CHRISTMAS!
HELLO CHRISTMAS
MERRY CHRISTMAS!
MERRY CHRISTMAS!
Merry Christmas!

MERRY CHRISTMAS
Colour in the snowman

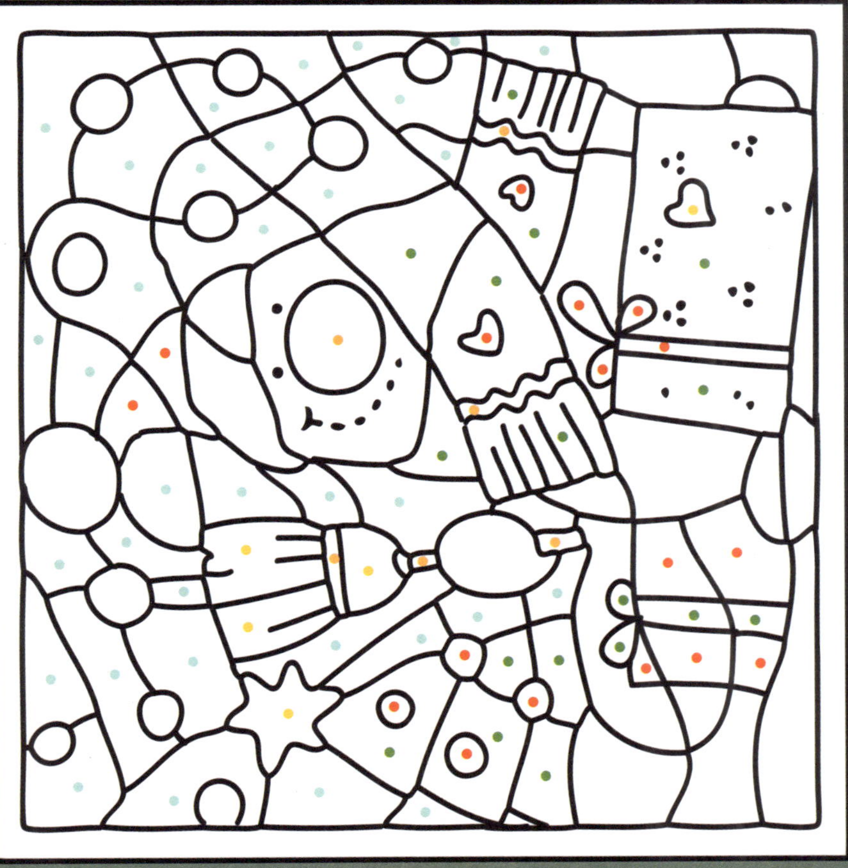

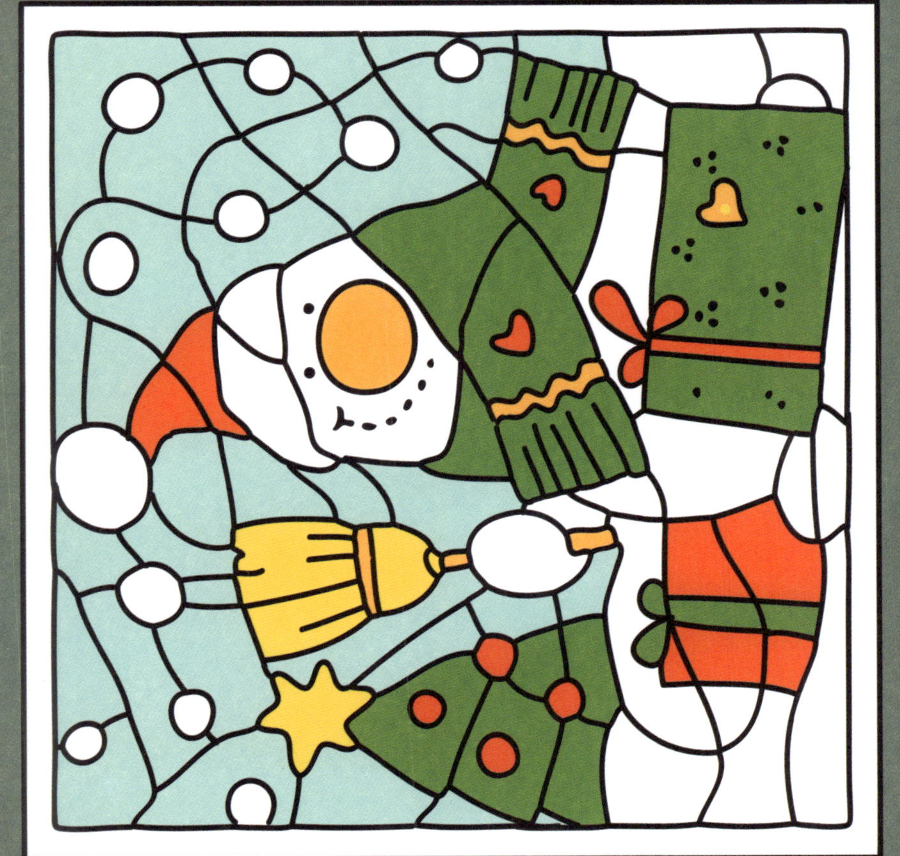

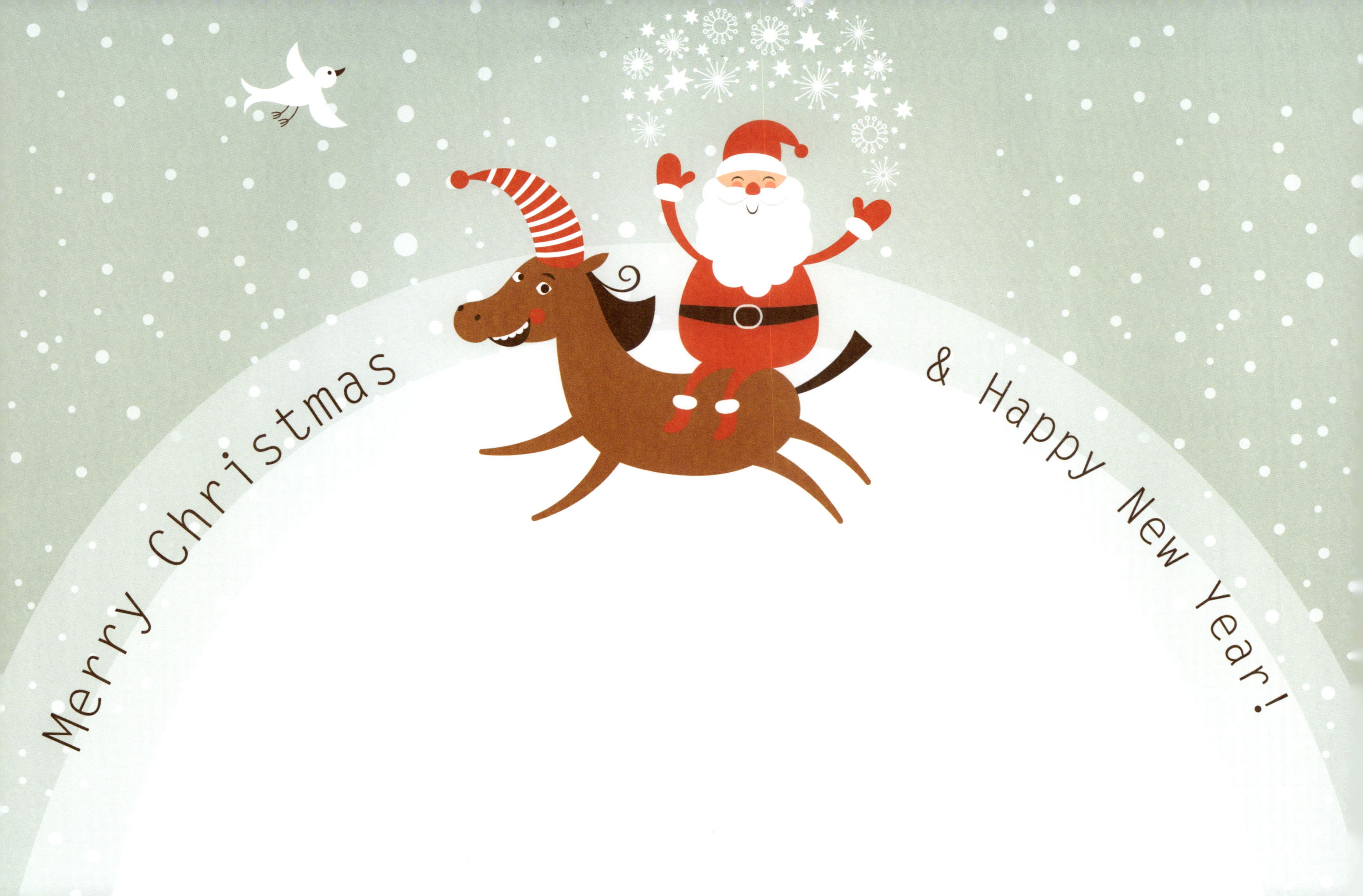

Merry Christmas
& Happy New Year!

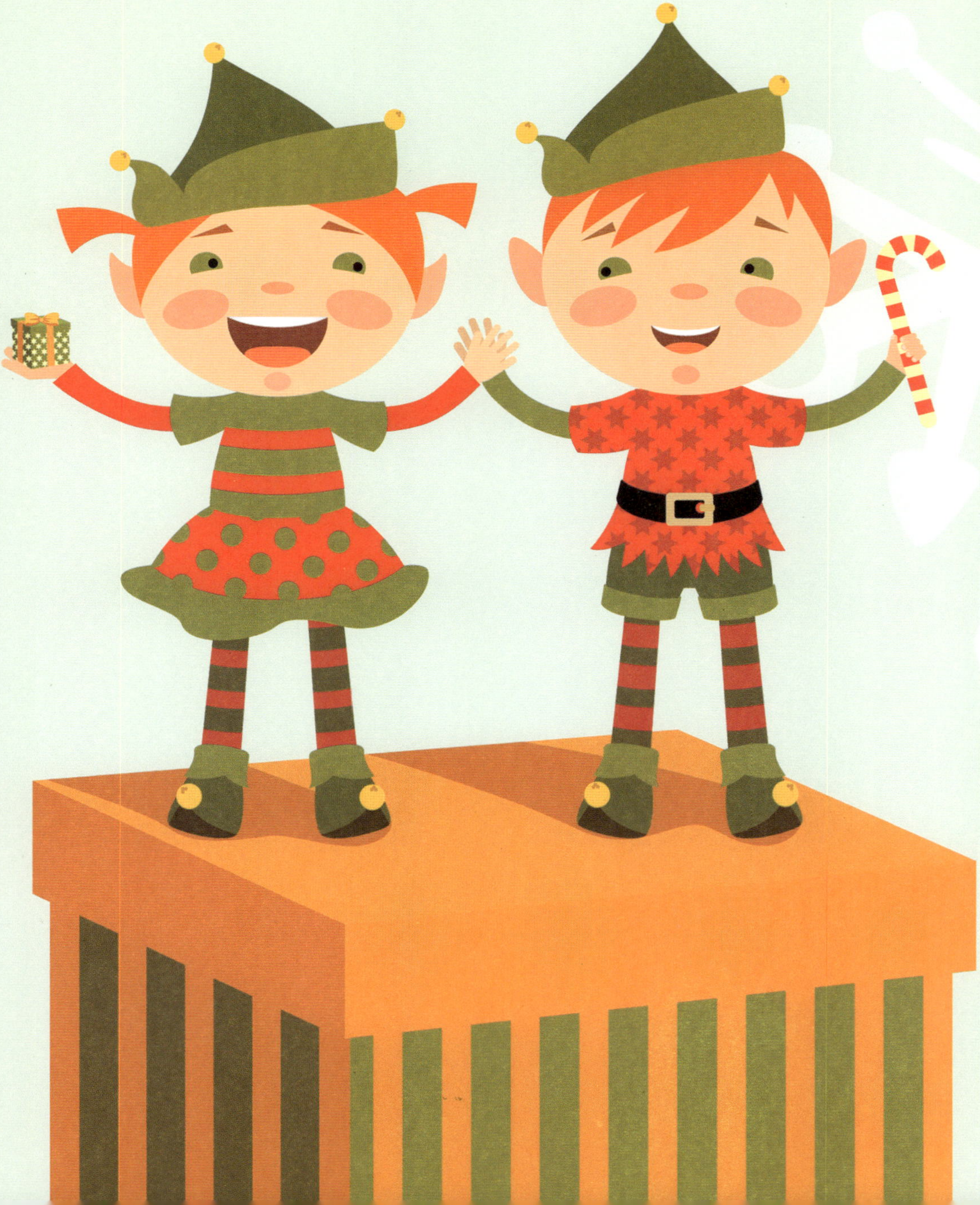

Will you be helping Santa this year?
Draw a picture of you as an elf!

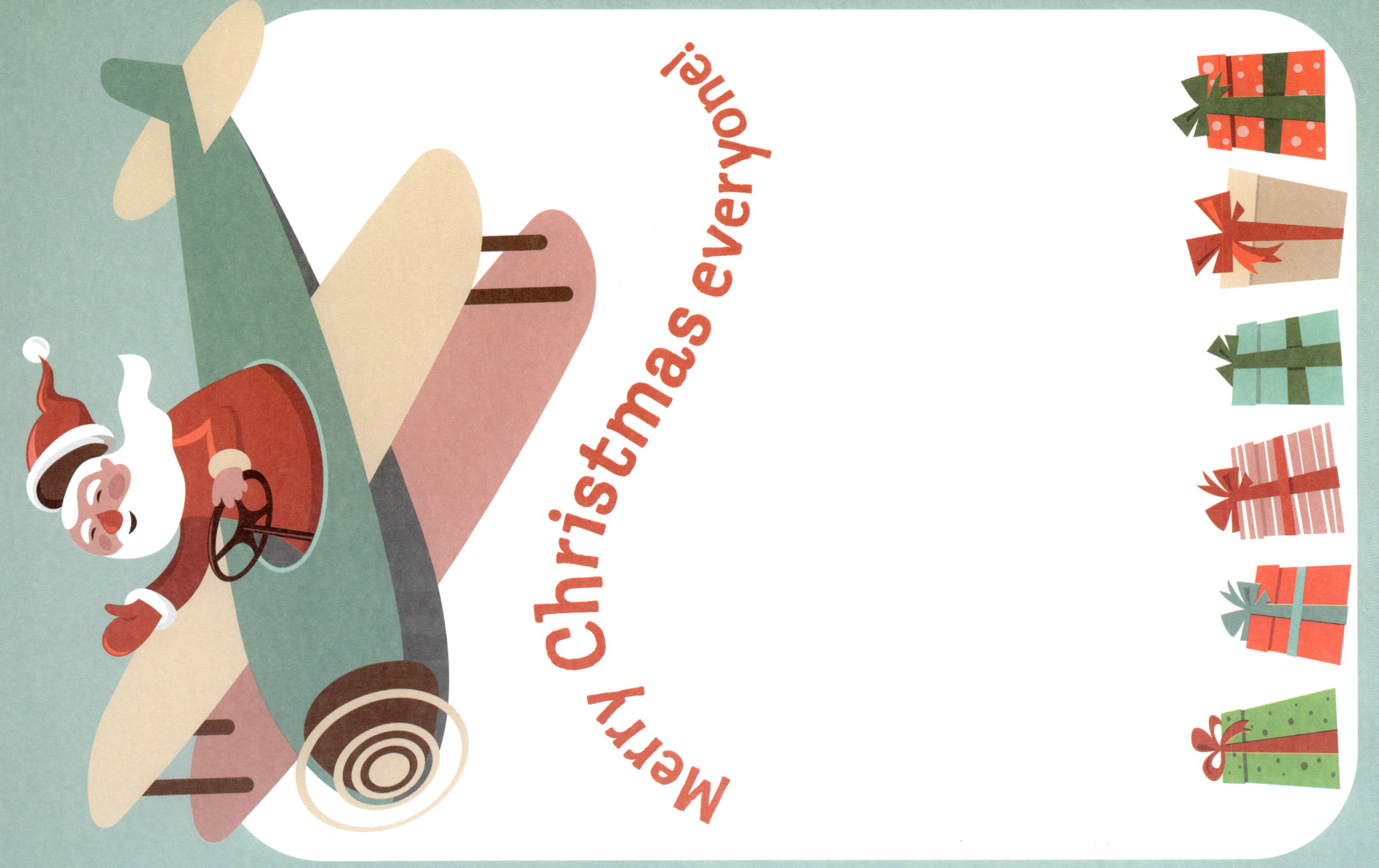

Merry Christmas everyone!

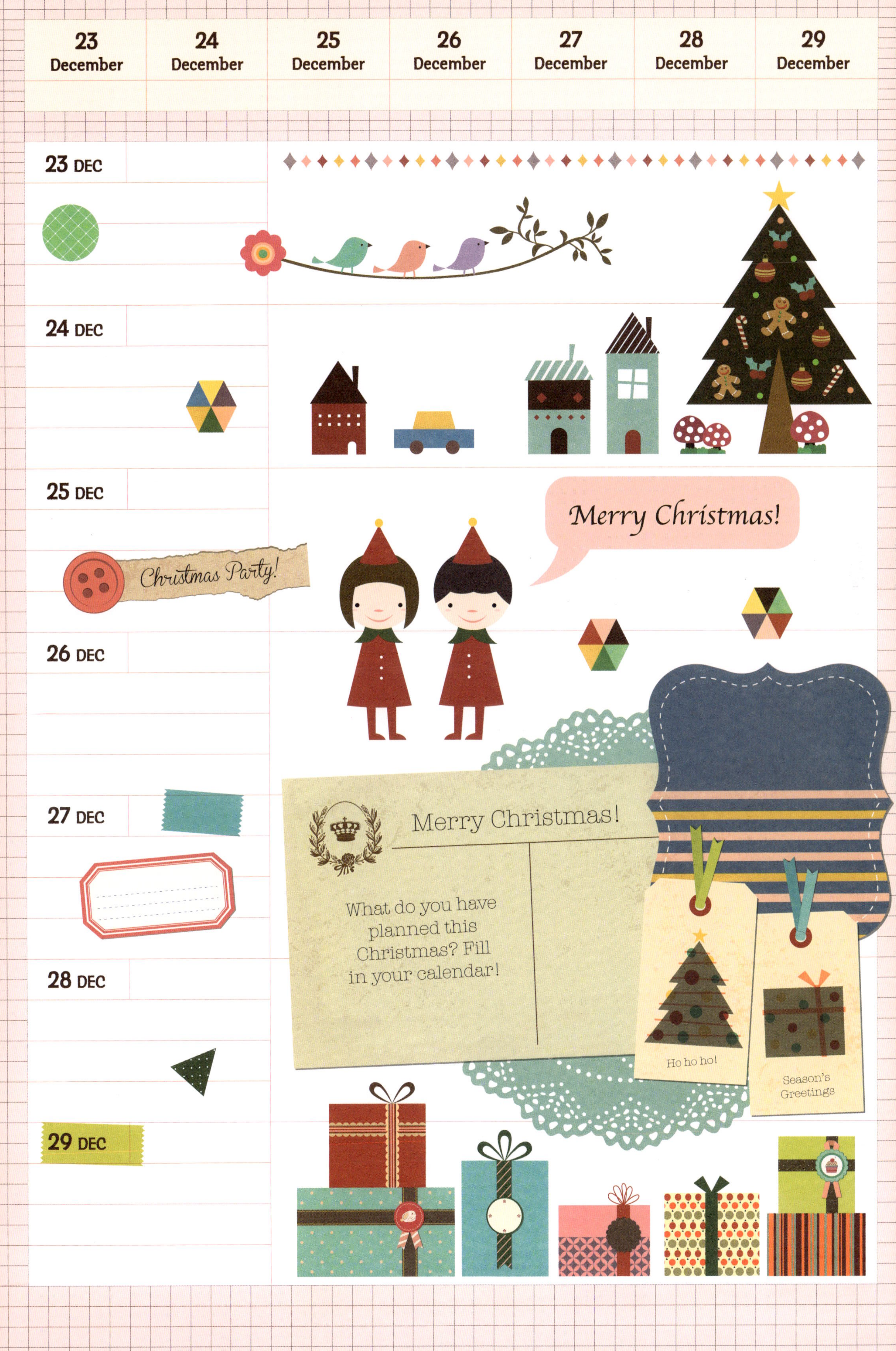

23 December
24 December
25 December
26 December
27 December
28 December
29 December
23 DEC
24 DEC
25 DEC
26 DEC
27 DEC
28 DEC
29 DEC
Christmas Party!
Merry Christmas!
Merry Christmas!
What do you have planned this Christmas? Fill in your calendar!
Ho ho ho!
Season's Greetings

Merry Christmas

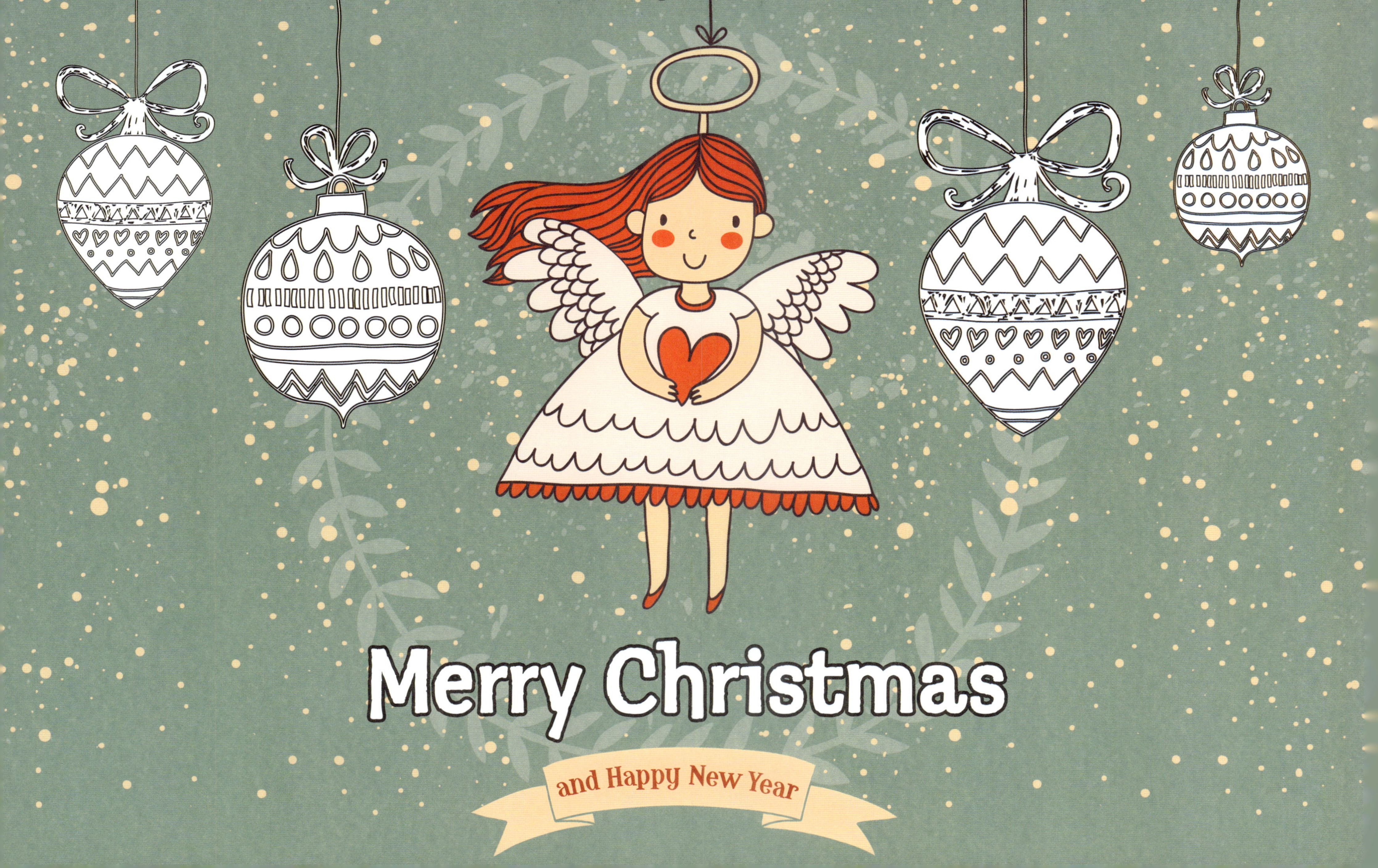

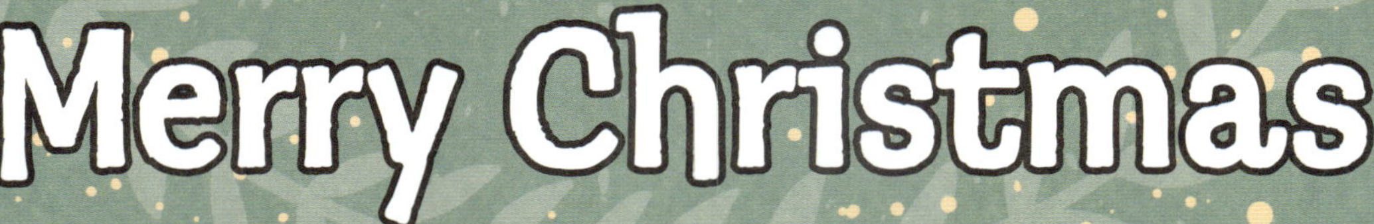

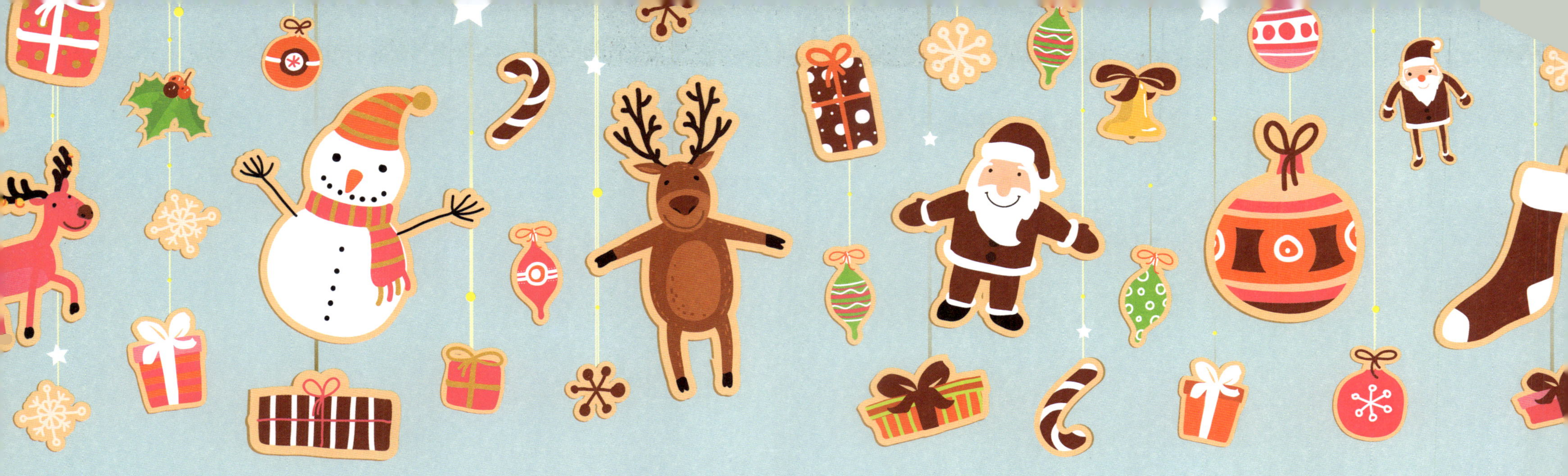

Draw a holiday picture here